Marbling

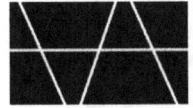

Marbling ©2022 by **Dani Tauber**. Published in the United States by Vegetarian Alcoholic Poetry, LLC. Not one part of this work may be reproduced without written consent from the author. Not one part of you is real. For more information, please write V.A. Poetry, 643 South 2nd Street, Milwaukee, WI 53204

Cover art by Jessi Carrubba

oh! - to die alone
at the end of a long
and sad life fraught
with constant trauma,
and disappointment,
and grief, after having
dedicated yourself
to caring for people
who did not deserve
it until you were just so
withered and decrepit
you could hardly stand.
to not be found, until
later-enough for your
blood to have pooled
at the points where
your fragile body
touched the dirty floor,
marbling so beautifully
under the skin.

you think that if you stay
completely still for too long
you will be able to feel yourself
decay - your stomach bloats
and your skin slips. your teeth
crumble, your tongue swells,
your eyes sink into themselves.
you sleep on your back with
your hands folded across
yourself, for the practice.

no one knows me, just the
leanest, most digestible parts.
there is rarely gristle or bone.
no one ever seems to have the
time to just really sit and eat
                    anymore.

exactly how many ghosts
flew out of my mouth and
eyes once i hit the pavement
after the fall? did anyone see?
did they look well fed?

i am a raw, exposed nerve; i don't ever heal because i keep picking at my scabs.

my past selves are buried in cheap, shallow graves and sometimes when it rains too hard, their toes or their noses or the tops of their folded hands become visible again.

i've stopped looking in mirrors because
the eyes are the windows to the soul and
i am terrified of what's inside. i am a haunted
house, with ghosts watching themselves
swing from the rafters and ghosts standing
over themselves bled out or electrocuted
in porcelain claw bathtubs and ghosts
trying to pull their heads out of ovens
because heavens, it's almost lunchtime
and ghosts sitting next to themselves
slumped over the steering wheels in cars
in garages filled with smoke and oh god
in the walls and the floors and even
the foundation, so much fucking rot.

the gray days are the most difficult;
the days when nothing really feels
real - least of all you. it's a different
kind of quiet, a different kind of cold
and both of them, piercing. time feels
viscous, it's hard to move through so
you stay in bed most of the day to save
your energy, your strength. lotta gray
days ahead, you know. winter again.
december's breath on the back of your
neck and you, baby born in a blizzard.

an ocean can pretend to be small
and tell itself it's a tide pool all it
wants but it will always be deep
and overflowing and dark and
there's so much, in there.

i'm locked in a room that is
you and i keep throwing myself
at this big, heavy door that is
also you - over and over and over -
and what i think i want is in, but
what i desperately need is out.

it's a different kind of anger, now.
it's not an early 20's pissed off and
lovesick fucking reading bukowski on
public transit on your way to let some
punk feel you up even though he
doesn't think you two are "like that"
try to cry in the shower later but can't.
it's more of a forest fire in a fucking
                ashtray.

sometimes when the ache gets really bad
i think it must be because i've been alive
longer than i was ever supposed to be; i think
maybe i should have just done the humane
thing instead of letting myself fall in love,
or know success, or think i had any kind of
                    right to happiness.

the image i hold onto hardest in my
memory of the days before it all went
to shit is of pink cigarettes. the french
ones, with the roses, snuck over the
canadian border in a coat with lots of
flowers on it. before the turbulent flight
and the boy who broke my fucking heart
and the anxiety i lost all control over and
all the fucking mistakes over the years
that followed up to this point, pink cigarettes.
i will never hold the expensive, gorgeous
french ones in my shaking fingers again.
the coat with the flowers is long lost.
i think about buying nat sherman's for the
hell of it, maybe to prove they're not bad luck.
maybe to be able to say, 'i told you so,'
when it all falls back to shit again just like
i've been dreading it will because things are
too good and something shattering will have
to balance the scale back out. pink cigarettes
and a rattling in my chest that says,' you're
gonna lose everything that ever mattered
to you, whether you throw it away yourself in
big black trash bags on your way up and out
or your house burns down for fucking trying it.'

at a certain point, no one comes
when you cry anymore. i don't
know. maybe you just get
        quieter
            or
                something.

in sixth grade they took you out of
science class and made you talk to the
psychiatrist at school-based youth
services because you related too much
to the worn-down rock faces in the
erosion unit. you started crying quietly
and couldn't seem to stop yourself.
but it wasn't just canyons, plateaus.
a worn spot of paint on something
touched frequently always hurt too.

even our smallest, most innocuous coping mechanisms are targeted attacks on ourselves whether we realize them or not, i think as i sip hot chocolate from a mug that says austin, tx. i have never been there, i just bought it for 25 cents at a thrift store. just like every other mug from someplace i've never fucking been that just happened to be 25 cents at a thrift store, thanks to my little self-preserving habit of buying fucking mugs from places i've never fucking been and won't ever go to, just so every day i feel like i actually have someplace to run to, if i had to.

i am told that god never
gives us more than we can
handle and i have to wonder
if maybe his expectations
of me are too high; i have to
assume that if i am made in
his image, he's a fuck-up too.

you could die tomorrow,
and what difference would
it fucking make, if you hadn't
been living to begin with?

capillaries fill with blood,
flushing your chest bright
like a robin in the steaming
shower where you think
about all the times he hurt
you and how easy you
made it for him. you sigh.
not all warmth is safe.
you never should have
traded being careful
for being cared for.

with my hip bones ground into the porcelain of the sink and my face pressed up against the mirror's cold glass i feel useful; on the walk home i think about how the cherry of my cigarette looks like a phantom light i'm following to some certain death and i smile because, if only. if only.

i will die in this house i will die
right here - dirty bathroom floor,
filmy mirror reflection of one pale
wrist exposed upward so delicately.
my heart will give out and my body
will give up but you know, god knows
i could really use the fucking rest.

the skeleton of something small but
deadly lives up high in my rib cage,
wraps its bone-fingers around my
heart and squeezes. it used to scare
me; now it's the only thing i can count on.
it is familiar, it is dependable, it is mine.

in a black and white movie scene
an elegant woman slaps herself
across the face to stifle her tears.
the sudden shock allows her to
recalibrate and compose herself.
when i do it, i just end up crying
                      harder.

i don't have a plan for if i should overcome - if i fall in love with life and lose the philosophy that keeps me here. sometimes i allow myself to think about my potential, if i were ever to get out of here and finally live up to it, but it's usually just to punish myself.

i'm a glacier.
i'm in amber.
i'm in a snow globe.
i'm in the bell jar.
i'm numb, i'm numb,
i'm numb.

dani tauber is a messy poet and former music journalist from southern new jersey. she has been published and / or shared by and in vegetarian alcoholic press, apep publications, resurrection magazine, heartworm press, moonchild magazine, and pink plastic press among others, as well as writing rock-n-roll adivce column MEDIOxCORE for the aquarian weekly for several years. her first full length poetry collection 'just like soft fruit' was released by vegetarian alcoholic press in february of 2021. she also runs vulnerary magazine.

i think it's time i said goodbye.
the wound is no longer warm,
inviting for tiny anxious fingers.
the scab ripened and ripped ages
ago, and the soft, pink scar that
used to be so pretty is now just
boring and familiar. the pain is
predictable, stale - now just a
dull ache where a deep, burning
void once was. i've been due for
some healing; i think it's time i
                said goodbye.

i think i could sleep here. through
the night, even. maybe. i think so.
i think i could learn to cook and
take care of myself here. really
thrive, really live up to some of
that potential i had so much
of when i was a kid. imagine?
i think i could write here, write
a few more books and some
songs. i could make a record
here. i think i could relax here
and get railed four times in
one night here and take my
time getting everything just
right, just exactly how i want
it here. i think i could unlearn
a lot here, think i could form
some healthier habits and
learn to be fearless here. i've
never wanted anything more.

i've been a bit afraid of myself lately; i have never felt so strong in my power before. i've processed a lot and let go of a lot more and i'm feeling so much grief and rage, but there's so much hope and excitement too. the old me is dead and buried in the backyard, but the new me isn't crawling yet, can't even really hold her head upright. it is equally draining and liberating, to grow into yourself. an ache in the bones for life.

i wanted to be so many things,
when i was small: an egyptologist,
a marine biologist, a movie star.
my parents had their hopes. instead
i grew up to be the human embodiment
of a fucking roadside memorial.
beautiful and tragic, all at once.
probably hard to look at.

my mother saved and carried so much but
everything will eventually be thrown away.
things you need, things you love, things
you never dreamed of living without.
things you're proud of. things that used
to keep you up at night. special things
that were given to you by people who
aren't alive anymore, and the people too.
it all ends up getting thrown away -
whether you do it yourself, hauling the
wreckage of your life to the fucking curb
in big black trash bags, or some other sorry
son of a bitch has to deal with it when you die.

they compare me to a phoenix, every time
my life burns down and i rebuild after the fire.
thirty-two years and no one's noticed i've been
rebuilding only from what could be salvaged
from the wreckage - over and over and over
again - all burnt out shells of what things
used to be, what things used to mean. i am
so fucking tired of hearing about the phoenix.
                              i am so fucking tired.

starved hope and naked rage
sit across from each other and
take turns spitting in each others'
mouths. on the small table between
them is a box full of trauma, curated
and collected over a brutal lifetime:
photographs and mementos and
train tickets, memories of good times
that were never actually good. the
things saved from the fire, the things
scavenged from the wreckage.
starved hope drags her jagged
fingernails across the table,
shredding the laminate right off.
naked rage laughs without blinking.
the box putrefies and decays.
ugly truth is written in their bones,
fullest potential sits under the table,
hugging herself and rocking back
and forth. screaming with no sound.
a wish
        starts to grow
                from the rotting box.
but nothing survives long in here.

i write in lowercase
because i'm always
w h i s p e r i n g .
sometimes a prayer.
sometimes a curse.

i grew up apologetic for and ashamed of
my ugliness - especially when laughing,
when talking - my awful side profile and
my crooked teeth and sloppy smile. i grew
up looking into mirrors and hating what i
saw, learned much later, long after i'd
assumed i'd "bloomed" how to cultivate
and curate myself into something more
ethereal than hideous. held the pose
for as long as i could; held the pose
for decades. but these days somehow
joy is leaking back in, through all the
cracks in the foundation. i can't help it.
i see a candid photo of myself that
would have upset me years ago and i
just have to fucking laugh, again,
unpretty as shit, thinking about how
fairies don't actually look the way they
are portrayed. they're horrid, rotten
little things with sharp, crooked teeth
and sharp, crooked elbows and knees
and wild hair all full of knots just like mine.
my ugliness is primal, elemental, mythical.
my prettiness is manufactured, is a glamor.
i'm so powerful that neither fucking matters.

fourteen years, since you died
and i didn't. fractured into halves,
that's seven and seven. i remember
reading somewhere that it takes
seven years for all the cells of the
body to die off and regenerate.
i am two whole physical selves
removed from fourteen years ago.
so how am i still stuck here?

the phone rarely rings anymore
but when it does, it goes on until
the voicemail answers. it's just me
and that sound until it finally stops.
i don't listen to messages or return
calls. i've stopped answering texts.
i'm not sure what people actually
hear, when i tell them i'm unwell.
i've stopped answering the
question 'how are you' because
i don't feel like anyone really
gives a shit. i feel like no one
would notice my absence;
they barely seem to notice
                my presence.

used to be i was like a stupid puppy
always getting underfoot and stepped on
but always damn near pissing on the floor
with excitement every time i heard those
heavy work boots coming home and now
unsurprisingly i am feral and rabid and
when cornered or surprised i aim right
for the fucking throat and no one ever
wanted to hurt me, no, it just kinda
happened, over and over again, and
you know, no one's ever really surprised
by the fucking state i'm in these days
but damn do their eyes get wide
          when i bare my teeth.

"i'm sure you have so much to live for,
i can't walk away from this, i'm involved now,
let me help you," pleads the man who is
trying to keep the woman on the bridge from
jumping; "your life would be so much easier
if you didn't insert yourself into things that
have absolutely nothing to do with you,"
says the woman dead set on jumping.

sometimes the only kindness
i am capable of giving myself is
the reminder that i have a way
out of it all when i am panicking,
the reminder that i am actually
in complete control after all.

i keep hurting myself
with the things that i write
but it's an exorcism so
maybe that's the point.
maybe i'm just doing it right.

isn't it so convenient,
being able to explain
away you never bringing
a life into this world by
referencing and blaming
"the way things are these
days?" never having to
admit that you're not sure
you're capable of nurturing,
of caring for, of caring about…
never having to admit that
the only child you could
ever see yourself loving
and protecting and cleaning
up after is the one that's
been inside of you all along,
the one who should have
had a chance to become.

people like to believe that the truth
will set you free but i'm not convinced;
i think you're more free the moment
you decide you no longer need to know.
you're free once you relieve yourself
of wondering, of caring whether or not
the people in your life who hurt you
feel bad about any of it and accepting
                      that they probably don't.

the ghost up in the window is me.
in every photograph taken from the
street, the driveway, the yard since
1989 with the swollen face and wet,
heavy eyes and messy hair looking
down longingly at whatever small
happiness was occurring below,
sad knowing it was never for her.
the ghost up in the window has
always been me; i was the draft in
this house long before i was dead
                                    and buried.

i will miss the smell of the bay's
low tide on the summer breeze if
i ever leave this house, or, i suppose,
i will smell it forever if i die in here.

i suppose when my parents die
i'll mostly mourn who they weren't,
who they didn't get to be. i hope to hell
there's no one left to do the same
for me when i go; no one to sift through
the wreckage of my life wondering
what happens to all that potential.
does it go in the ground? do they leave
room in the urn, for it to settle on top
of the bone dust like black mold,
sitting in the back of a dark closet
next to your father's gun for however
long until someone finally remembers
to dump it into the deep blue sea?

my body is a tomb, a monument
to every trauma ever inflicted upon it.
a roadside memorial for everything
i could have been if i'd ever in my
life had what i'd needed. my body
is shrapnel and broken glass, the
smell of gas and gravel and tiny
teeth, stuck in concrete. wings
that might have opened up before
impact if they'd grown in right,
instead malnourished and weak;
underdeveloped and so small.

i don't wear a bra or dye my
hair anymore and sometimes i
don't shave my legs, either.
i still treat makeup and clothing
like battle armor, still only wear
jewelry that feels talismanic or
is sharp enough to draw blood
if need be. i have learned to
love my sun freckles, my
crooked teeth, my exhausted
and broken body that still
carries every scar, bruise, and
bleeding wound that was ever
inflicted upon it on the inside
as well as the battered outside.
i have learned to coexist
peacefully with everything
that i am and everything that
i should have been and everything
that i am not or just couldn't
live up to. i have forgiven so much.
i am still kind, in spite of it all, but
i have also learned to lock doors.
i fucked up my hands real bad
trying to hold onto too much
but i can still write, and so i do.
it used to scare me that my words
were all i had but now it's a comfort.
words are all i need, now. i haven't
had to prove anything in years.

it'll happen, someday. it has to.
we will lock eyes across some
moderately crowded bar, or at
some house show, and you'll
look for it - the contempt, the
resentment, the hatred - but
you'll only see, for a brief
moment, pity. then the honest
sorrow of mourning what we
both know would have been.
and it'll end up hurting you
far more than it hurts me.
and i will look away first.

it's july and everyone is
commenting on my tan like
i'm all better now. like i'm
somehow healthy, happy now.
like they were right all along and
all i ever needed was a little
sun, like my father's potted plants,
to be cured of the ghosts in my
head and the tragedy in my blood…
as if by winter i won't wither and die
like so many past flowers and ferns.

what am i, to you...?
the cricket in your floor.
the thorn in your paw.
the arrow in your side.
the shrapnel in your ribs.
the leak of your faucet.
the draft in your bedroom.
the ticking of your clock.
the fly in your soup.
the crack in your foundation.
the mosquito in your ear.
the dirt under your rug.
the blood in your sink.
the knife on your plate.
the dull ache that won't
                      go away.

why wait until
you're dead and
gone to start
haunting people?

ex ossibus

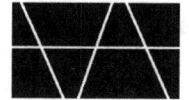

ex ossibus ©2022 by **Dani Tauber**. Published in the United States by Vegetarian Alcoholic Press. Not one part of this work may be reproduced without written consent from the author, unless you're doing something really rad with it. For more information, please write V.A. Poetry, 643 South 2nd Street, Milwaukee, WI 53204

Cover art by Jessi Carrubba